IT'S
YOUR SIZE

It's Your Size

If God allows it to come your way, it's because He knows you can handle it.

ANTHONY ADEFARAKAN

GLOEM, CANADA

CONTENTS

~ ~

Dedication

1

~ ~

Acknowledgement

3

~ ~

Introduction

5

~ chapter one ~

WHAT ARE PROBLEMS?

7

~ chapter two ~

THE CAUSES OF PROBLEMS

11

~ chapter three ~

THE EFFECTS OF PROBLEMS

15

~ chapter four ~
OVERCOMING PROBLEMS
21

~ ~

Prayer Points
35

~ ~

Become a Financial Partner with Jesus
37

~ ~

About the Author
39

DEDICATION

I dedicate this book to God Almighty for His goodness and faithfulness in making His Word available to me. All glory to His Holy Name.

Also to everyone facing one challenge or the other, I stand with you all and decree that you are coming out stronger in Jesus' Name.

ACKNOWLEDGEMENT

I sincerely acknowledge my Eternal Father, Who alone is the Source of all wisdom. He is the Author and Finisher of my faith and it is of His fullness that the contents of this book have been drawn.

Also, I want to profoundly appreciate my dear parents – Prince and Mrs. Timothy Adefarakan – for bringing me up in the way of the Lord and for instilling righteousness consciousness in me. The wonderful education foundation I was given, coupled with their constant encouragement has empowered me to reach heights that were once beyond my imagination.

My most special appreciation goes to my sweetheart, Abisolami; without her help and support I would never have enjoyed the conducive atmosphere needed to publish this book. I appreciate your love, encouragement, and the support you give at all times. Thank you so much. I love you my Baby!

To Pastor C.T Oni of the Redeemed Christian Church of God, thanks so much for going through the manuscript and offering wonderful guidance towards its success. And to all my other mentors in Ministry, I appreciate you all. Your investments in my life are not in vain. May the Lord reward you all in Jesus' Name.

INTRODUCTION

Problems are inevitable as far as man's life is concerned; and they come in diverse forms. But unfortunately, many people's negative reaction to them is what makes the purpose unaccomplished and shattered.

Jesus Christ said *"...in the world you shall have tribulation, but be of good cheer, I have overcome the world"* (John 16:33). So we are not expected to see it strange when we face any form of tribulation; rather we are to take the bull by the horn and approach them with an overcomer's mindset, as running away from them may bring about falling into other ones. It has been said that the best form of defense is to attack. Thus, problems are to be challenged face-to-face and overcome so as to move ahead.

However, there are certain information we need to possess before we can successfully challenge and overcome our troubles. 1 Corinthians 10:13 says *'There has no temptation taken you but such as is common to man, but God is faithful, who will not allow you to be temped above that you are able but will with the temptation also make a way of escape that you may be able to bear it.'* In other words, the Word of God is saying that your condition is not beyond you; and that you are well able to handle it.

In Fashion designing, clothes are not sown for people without first taking their measurements into consideration. That is, a tailor will not sow a piece of cloth for you if your size (measurement) is unknown to him. In the same way, God will never allow you to face any challenge that is more than your size and strength; and it is this fundamental understanding that will assist you in taking the appropriate measures as outlined in this book towards combating every form of problem that comes your way.

I pray as you read on, God's overcoming grace will rest upon you in Jesus' Name.

Anthony Adefarakan.

~ Chapter One ~

WHAT ARE PROBLEMS?

According to Oxford Advanced Learner's Dictionary, a problem is defined as a thing that is difficult to deal with or to understand. So from this definition, it could be inferred that problems have to do with difficulties. They are unfavorable situations that befall people; and they can also be called **predicaments, afflictions, tribulations, troubles, challenges** etc depending on their nature.

One thing that is however worthy of note is the fact that no living being can exist on this planet without encountering one problem or the other; regardless of how well-meaning. As a matter of fact, Jesus Christ confirmed this assertion when He said in John 16:33 that in the world His disciples would have tribulation. He didn't say 'you may have tribulation'; rather He said 'you shall have tribulation'. So problems are inevitable as long as you are still living in this world.

Examples of problems many people face in this world include:

Barrenness

This is a state of being unproductive; and it may be mental – a dull brain; financial – a state of lack; or marital – childlessness. Anyone facing these kinds of situations can be said to have a problem. In the scriptures, Sarah, Hannah, Rachael among others suffered this fate at certain stages of their lives. [Genesis 16:1-3; 1 Samuel 1:1-16; and Genesis 29:31 respectively].

Sickness

This is a state of illness or bad health. A sick fellow is obviously not comfortable; and to such a person, sickness is their problem. This sickness may also be financial in nature. A financially sick fellow has a sickness called poverty; and it is a very major problem facing many people in the world today. Examples of people who experienced sickness at one time or the other in the scriptures are Peter's Mother-in-law [Luke 4:38], Lazarus [John 11:2-3], the impotent man at the pool of Bethesda [John 5:1-5] among others.

Deformity

This can either be internal or external. The physically challenged people e.g. the lame, the blind, the deaf, the dumb etc are faced with predicaments. Such people are not comfortable with their situations, they may just have to learn to live with them.
The internally deformed are challenged as well. For instance, I once heard of a man who had big feminine breasts and even menstruated. What an ordeal! Examples of deformed people in the Bible include the woman with the issue of blood [Mark 5: 25-26], the man who was born blind [John 9:1-3], the lame man at the Beautiful Gate [Acts 3:2-3] among others.

Faulty Foundations

Some people's problems are rooted in their family foundations. There are men and women who have been dedicated to family gods and goddesses; and because they don't serve them as a result of religious beliefs or civilization, their lives begin to witness one form of calamity or the other. Foundational problems run at the very root of the family and mostly affect all the children born in that family. It is a problem.

Losses

These may be due to bankruptcy or natural disasters such as flood, violent wind, storms, earthquakes, tsunamis, volcanic eruptions etc. All these may result in the death of loved ones, destruction of valuable property, loss of wealth among other unfavorable outcomes. Anyone caught in any of these conditions is definitely faced with difficulties. Can you imagine a 65 years old widow losing her only son in a ghastly motor accident? Now that is a pain only God would be able to soothe.

Ignorance

This is a very serious problem. And worse enough, many people with this problem don't even know they have a problem. It is a state of lack of knowledge; and Hosea 4:6 says it can lead to destruction. Many have died of ignorance and that's a terrible fact. Ignorance of any kind is a problem.

These are just to mention a few. There are diverse kinds of problems facing mankind; and even Christians experience these at one point or the other in their walk with God. But noteworthy is Psalm 34:19 which says *"Many are the afflictions of the righteous, but the Lord delivers him out of them all."* That is, there is provision for deliverance.

~ Chapter Two ~

THE CAUSES OF PROBLEMS

Problems are caused by so many factors; but Biblically, two broad causes are recognized. They are:

1. Man, and
2. The Devil.

Now let's consider them.

Man
Problems are caused by men (humans) through lustful desires, carelessness, disobedience, rebellion, indiscipline among others. In this case, men fall into various troubles when drawn away by their selfish interests.

For instance, a man who practices conjugal infidelity would certainly not be justified to blame the devil when he eventually falls into the trap of HIV/AIDS – an incurable disease.

Also, a civil servant who spends more than he earns is expressly inviting the temptation to borrow which if not properly managed will land him in indebtedness. And if on the other hand, such a fellow decides to start stealing public funds or begins to engage in other fraudulent acts, he would eventually be caught and most likely be dismissed from public service, thus rubbishing all his years of hard labor.

By the time this happens, suspecting one witch somewhere for his predicament would be very unfair; seeing that he brought it upon himself. And it all started with indiscipline and greed. Such are the problems caused by man.

James 1:13-15 says *"Let no man say when he is tempted, I am tempted of God; for God cannot be tempted with evil, neither tempts He any man. But every man is tempted when he is drawn away of his own lust and enticed. Then when lust has conceived, it bring forth sin, and sin, when it is finished brings forth death."*

A typical example of this is found in Acts 5:1-10, when Ananias and Sapphira brought death sentence upon themselves by lying to the Holy Spirit. If they had told the truth, they would have lived.

Man can also cause problems in other people's lives. God said the heart of man is desperately wicked (Jeremiah 17:9). We have heard of some wicked people who through some diabolical means lock up women's wombs, preventing them from conceiving; and thereby causing barrenness in such lives. Also, some kill innocent people for political or business reasons thereby bringing grief, pain and irreparable loss to their victims' families. These are man-made predicaments.

As we read earlier, the Bible says God doesn't tempt anyone. So it is advisable to be self-disciplined and control our appetites. Let's stop running after vanities; it is very unwise to forget to live while trying to make a living. Let us allow contentment to guide our dealings so as not to bring problems upon ourselves and upon others around us.

The Devil

As a matter of fact, this is the tempter himself. He designs, manufactures and channels temptations into the lives of men. There are instances in the Scriptures when the devil tempted men.

Job was a perfect example of someone who suffered in the hands of Satan. The greater part of the book of Job relates the ordeals brought upon him by the devil. He seriously dealt with Job until his wife preferred being a widow to watching him suffer. She literally told him to curse God and die. The devil attacked his health, sheep, oxen, gold, silver, children etc. He was evidently devastated. The experience of Job clearly points out what the devil can do to a man if allowed.

Also, according to Genesis 3:1-7, man fell from grace to grass; and from glory to shame because of what the devil did. This problem of sin as introduced by the devil is still destroying many people's destinies today; especially those who have not yet run to Jesus Christ for refuge – Proverbs 18:10.

The devil is man's chief adversary and his main aim in all the problems he causes is to draw man's attention away from his Maker. And when that happens, he takes over completely.

He displays the pleasures of sin but hides the price tag. He brings overwhelming problems so man can start seeing God as wicked. Satan is a trouble maker; you must never yield to his wiles. Remember, temptation is not yet a sin until you yield to it.

~ Chapter Three ~

THE EFFECTS OF PROBLEMS

Nothing happens by chance; there is always a reason and purpose for every occurrence in life - problems inclusive.

However, these occurrences could either have positive or negative effects. When they result in a fall, they are negative; but when they eventually lead to a rising or promotion, then they are positive.

Let's consider these effects in detail;

Negative Effects of Problems

These happen when problems are not properly handled. In this case, such problems can lead to sin; especially when one begins to seek help from ungodly sources like consulting witch doctors, occult groups etc.

Also, problems can weigh one's spirit down when they become so overwhelming; and if they remain unsolved for a long period of time, the resultant hopelessness may actually bring suicide into the picture. Such are the negative effects problems can have on a person.

Positive Effects of Problems

These happen when problems are handled the right way. Here, the God-factor is taken into consideration that nothing happens on earth without His adequate knowledge. The Bible says the very hairs of our heads are numbered and not one of them drops without His notice. Also, in Lamentations 3:37 the Bible says *"Who is he that says, and it comes to pass when the Lord commands it not?"*

God is omniscient and He thus knows all things. Although He doesn't tempt any man (according to James 1:13), He sometimes allows it (Job 1:12). Even in the case of His only begotten Son, Jesus Christ, He organized it as seen in Matthew 4:1 – *"Then was Jesus led up by the Spirit into the wilderness to be tempted by the devil"*. Nothing catches God unawares. But unlike the devil, God allows the various problems, troubles, and temptations that come our way for good and constructive purposes.

So, in your predicament as a child of God, He's just trying to say 'My dear, before you can be promoted, you will have to undergo some tests and examinations so that you can be fit to occupy the next level being prepared for you. It wasn't designed for your fall.'

The problems you are facing now may just be a test targeted at checking your emotional strength, maturity, consistency, patience among other qualities necessary for your growth. Your circumstances should make you depend on God, rather than making you feel He doesn't care.

Consider the following Characters from Scriptures:

1. Jesus Christ suffered in order to be able to help us (Christians) when we encounter sufferings (Hebrews 2:18; 4:15). He had to taste temptations and sufferings so as to know exactly what we are passing through and as a result offer a helping hand.
2. David suffered afflictions in order to learn God's statutes (Psalm 119:71).
3. Apostle Paul lived with a thorn in his flesh, a messenger of Satan sent to buffet him thereby preventing him from ex-

hibiting pride capable of destroying him. It was for his own good, and God's grace was made sufficient for him to be able to bear it (2 Corinthians 12:7-9).

4. The Red Sea and the fast approaching Egyptian host threw the children of Israel into utter despair. They were confused; and they thought all was over. But by the time God was through with them, the Red Sea opened up and the enemies they saw few hours ago all perished and they never saw them again. It was an arrangement made by God to get glory over Pharaoh and his host by drowning them (Exodus 14:1-31).

5. Esther was still very young when she lost her parents. Being an orphan, her uncle (Mordecai) took care of her and raised her up. As if being an orphan wasn't enough, she, together with her uncle, was captured and taken to a strange land as slaves. Life seemed so unfair to her. But when her time of visitation came, right in that strange land, God made her a queen and all her past sorrows were forgotten (Esther 2:5-18).

6. Daniel and his three Hebrew friends were taken to Babylon as captives, where they faced different kinds of ordeals. At a particular time, Daniel was thrown into the lions' den; and at another time, his friends (the three Hebrew boys) were thrown into a fiery furnace – all these happened to them because they refused to deny their God. They persisted in faith in the midst of their trials; and at the end, not only did God rescue and promote them to become Provincial Princes, He also used their experience to turn the hearts of the king and his people to Himself (Daniel 2:48 – 3:25). What a glorious ending!

7. Joseph was a man of destiny; and for that singular reason, he encountered various troubles. He was passionately hated by his own blood brothers; he was thrown into a pit,

sold into slavery, falsely accused by his master's wife, unjustly thrown into a prison and was forgotten for two years by someone he helped who could also help him get out of the prison. Worthy of mention is the fact that he also had painful injuries from the fetters and iron collars used on him while in the prison as stated in Psalm 105:18. Then there was the emotional pain of not seeing his father who loved him so much and thought he was dead for over a decade. Those were terrible moments in Joseph's life.

But then a day came and all his thirteen years of ordeal came to an abrupt end. There was a problem in the palace and the king got to know that Joseph's skill could solve it; so he sent for him and he was hastily transported to the palace. Upon proffering the much needed solution, he was made the First Prime Minister of Egypt when he was only 30 years of age.

He was being refined in those troubles as preparation for his greatness. And when the time was right, not only did he become great, he stayed great (Genesis 41:40-46).

8. Jephthah was the son of a prostitute; and as a result, he suffered rejection from his step-brothers. He was literally denied access to his father's possessions and was cast out of the family.

   Being an outcast, worthless men came to him and became his companions. He was living with an uncertain future in view. But a day came when the children of Ammon launched an attack against his city. His city people invited him to come and help them; so he obliged. He waged war against the enemies, defeated them and straight away became their captain (the head). His ordeal turned him into a captain (Judges 11:1-11).

9. Hannah was a woman of sorrow. She had a very great reproach called barrenness which made her a laughing stock;

and it seemed as if all her prayers were unheard by God. Her womb was shut.

Whereas her husband's other wife (Peninnah) already had children, she had none. Emotional pain and constant weeping characterized her life.

But then, her day finally came. God opened her womb and gave her a great prophet as her first son. Afterwards, she had five other children and her reproach finally ended in praise. She became the mother of Prophet Samuel – Israel's first king maker (1 Samuel 1:1-2:21).

10. Ruth was a widow who decided to follow her mother-in-law to her country. She left her own people and had to glean free grains behind the reapers to survive (with her aged mother-in-law). She experienced poverty in the real sense of the word. But at last, she met Boaz, got married again, and through her marriage she became one of the great ancestresses of Jesus Christ (Ruth 4:1-4). Her suffering landed her in fame and honor; her name entered Jesus' ancestry record in Matthew 1:5.

These are just to mention a few. But worthy of note is the fact that in all things, God has His plans and purposes. He knows the end right from the beginning.

Therefore, with this understanding, your predicament shouldn't call for pity or sympathy; God allowed it for a purpose which if patiently awaited would manifest at the appointed time. Only your knowledge-based endurance is required.

~ Chapter Four ~

OVERCOMING PROBLEMS

What happens to a man is not as important as how he reacts to it. Many have missed the plans of God for their lives just because they reacted wrongly to their circumstances.

As the Lord lives, your eyes will be opened in this chapter, and you will see the solutions to your present conditions in Jesus' Name.

<u>1 Corinthians 10:13 NKJV says</u> **_"No temptation has overtaken you except such as is common to man; but God is faithful, who will not allow you to be tempted beyond what you are able, but with the temptation will also make the way of escape, that you may be able to bear it."_**

Going by this verse, it means anytime you are faced with any challenge, difficulty, problem or the likes, certain facts should come alive in your mind. You must know that:

1. **<u>It is common</u>:** That is, you are not the only one in that condition. There is always someone somewhere experiencing the same thing. It is not peculiar to you. How consoling!
2. **<u>It is your size</u>:** That is, you can bear it. It is important to note here that God always measures His children's abilities before He allows any challenge or temptation to come their way. If it's allowed to come your way, you can be very sure your size has been considered. So cheer up, you can bear it.

3. **You are not alone.:** Isaiah 43:2 says "When you pass through the waters, I will be with you, and through the rivers, they shall not overflow you; when you walk through the fire, you shall not be burned, neither shall the flame scorch you." What a faithful God we serve! He was with those three Hebrew boys in the fiery furnace and was also with Joseph throughout his ordeals. He's the One Who said *'Fear not, for I am with you...'* (Isaiah 40:10). He delivered the children of Israel from the hands of Pharaoh and in Revelation 3:10, He promised to keep you from failing in the hour of testing. Nothing can separate you from His love; not even your problems (Romans 8:38-39). He is too faithful to fail. Don't ever forget that.

4. **Solutions always come with the problems:** That is, in every problem lies the solution. That verse says *"...but with the temptation will also make a way of escape..."* - so every time a problem strikes, its solution strikes with it.

   For instance in Numbers 21:5-9, poisonous snakes had been sent by God into the camp of the Israelites to punish them for their murmuring and complaining. At that moment they realized they had sinned and cried to Moses to help them beg God. Moses interceded for them and the solution God offered was for them to look at the bronze snake made by Moses as a replica of the ones biting them. What does that mean? Their problem was snake bite and the solution was to look at the snake made of bronze. Snake was still involved in their recovery.

   Also in 1 Samuel 17:50-51, the sword that brought down Goliath's head was his own. He came to the battle with the solution in his sheath; and when David discovered it, he simply used it to get rid of his head. David didn't have a sword; it was Goliath's sword that solved the problem caused by Goliath.

Be rest assured anytime you are faced with difficulties: the solution always comes with the package. Don't be nervous or anxious; be still, watch closely, and you will see the way out.

5. **It is temporal:** That is, it is not permanent: so you can't die in it. Psalm 30:5b says *"weeping may endure for a night, but joy comes in the morning"*. By the time God turned the captivity of Zion, the Bible says they were like them that dream (Psalm 126:1). It is a true saying that no condition is permanent.

    2 Corinthians 4:17 says *"For our light affliction which is but for a moment works for us a far more exceeding and eternal weight of glory"*. The longest time all your problems can last is 'a moment' compared to the season of joy awaiting you. The darkest part of the night has been said to be just before the dawn.

    Remember Jesus Christ in Hebrews 12:2? He endured the cross because He considered the whole suffering nothing but temporal compared to what awaited Him as recorded in Philippians 2:9-11. And as a result of His positive attitude to His sufferings, God promoted Him and gave Him a NAME THAT IS ABOVE EVERY OTHER NAME.

6. **Your promotion is imminent:** As we saw earlier, God has positive purposes for allowing the various trials and challenges that come into the lives of His children. And one of these purposes is promotion. No student is permitted to advance to higher classes of learning without taking an examination and passing it to show that they are capable of coping in the next class. Romans 8:28 says *"And we know that all things work together for good to them that love God, to them who are called according to His purpose."* In this life, there can't be testimonies without temptations; there can't be gain without pain; and there can't be glory without story.

It takes toughness to taste triumph; and sometimes, until they mock you, God may not make you. Job 23:10 says *"...when He has tested me, I shall come forth as gold."* No gold is appreciated or admired without it first experiencing the furnace. It is after the furnace experience that gold gets to be displayed for people to see; and only then can it attract a very good price. Why? It has become a highly valuable item (with the help of the fire). The knowledge and consciousness of these facts will help you approach any form of challenge or problem with optimism.

That being said, there are some conscious efforts you need to make in combating the challenges that come your way. I call these 'playing your part'.

Now, these measures are not to be applied in isolation but collectively. This is because they complement one another.

Here are the measures:

Surrender your life to Jesus Christ.

The importance of this cannot be overemphasized because He is the only One Who knows the end right from the beginning. He is the faithful One Who laid down His life for you even when you were neck deep in sin. He single-handedly carried the heaviest load that ever existed – the burden of sin.

This comes as the first measure because it is the determinant of the potency of the other measures.

Hebrews 2:3 says *"How shall we escape if we neglect so great a salvation..."* It is thus advisable you give your life to Jesus Christ and let Him paddle the canoe of your life if you really want to come forth as gold.

To go about this, go ahead and honestly confess your sins to Him; ask for His forgiveness with readiness to never return to them again; then call Him into your life, confessing Him as your Lord and Savior. As soon as you do this, He will take over your case and make sure it turns out for your good.

If you did that, congratulations! You are now saved. Guard your salvation jealously. It's your greatest asset in life.

Pray.

Prayer is the master key. Psalm 34:17 says *"The righteous cry, and the Lord hears, and delivers them out of all their troubles."* Also, Jeremiah 33:3 says *"Call unto me, and I will answer you..."*

Once you know you are in tune with God, the next thing to do is to pray; because He is the present help in time of trouble (Psalm 46:1).

There is a popular hymn that really expresses the benefits of prayer.

It goes thus;

What a friend we have in Jesus
All our sins and griefs to bear
What a privilege to carry
Everything to God in prayer
Oh, what peace we often forfeit
Oh, what needless pain we bear
All because we do not carry
Everything to God in prayer

Have we trials and temptations?
Is there trouble anywhere?
We should never be discouraged
Take it to the Lord in prayer
Can we find a friend so faithful
Who will all our sorrows share?
Jesus knows our every weakness
Take it to the Lord in prayer.

This hymn shows that indeed, Jesus is a faithful Friend. He is the One Who gave us a free invitation in Hebrews 4:16 which says *"Let us come boldly unto the throne of grace that we may obtain mercy and find grace to help in time of need."* In essence, He's saying 'My office is open; just walk straight in, make your requests and I will definitely help you.' But you will have to come in first: and that's done through prayer.

Hebrews 4:15 says *"For we have not a High priest who cannot be touched with the feeling of our weakness, but was in all points tempted like we are, yet without sin."* He has been through what you are currently passing through; so He knows the best way to help you if only you will call on Him. *"For in that He Himself suffered being tempted, He is able to help them that are tempted."* –Hebrews 2:18.

Prayer not only provides help in time of trouble, it also prevents you from entering into more temptations (Matthew 26:41). So you must pray to experience divine intervention rather than asking God "Why Me?"

Give God Praise.
Someone once said 'If you have lost anything, God is the reason you have not lost everything'.
You cannot correctly say God hasn't done anything for you; even if it's just for the fact that you are alive. You shouldn't be so overwhelmed by your problems that you fail to see the good things the Lord has done or is doing in your life. There is this quote that I like; it says "To be *thank full* is to be *praise full*, and to be *praise full* is to be *win full*". Anything that will take God takes praise.

Learn to worship Him and adore Him; say something good to Him and let Him know you are grateful for His past deeds in your life.
Be assured of this: if you praise God in your problem, He will definitely be moved to deliver you. Do you remember what Job did when he heard the news about the death of his children? The Bible

says he fell down upon the ground and worshipped (Job 1:20-22). You know what I have discovered? If you cannot worship God in your wilderness, you will not in your Canaan land. You've got to learn to appreciate God, bearing in mind that all things work together for your good and that your light affliction, which is but for a moment, cannot be compared to the eternal weight of glory awaiting you.

Did you know that no matter how big your problem is, it can't stop God from being God? So what's the issue? 1 Thessalonians 5:18 says *"In everything, give thanks; for this is the will of God for you in Christ Jesus."* And it is also written in John 16:33 that you should be of good cheer when faced with tribulation because He (Jesus) has conquered the world. For these beautiful promises and kind deeds of God towards you, He deserves your endless praises. Always remember that it is by focusing your attention on the past acts of God that you can get your present problems solved. That's how David solved the Goliath problem (1 Samuel 17:34-37).

Endure.
Persistence, they say, is the key to overcome resistance. James 1:2-4 says *"My brethren, count it all joy when you fall into various temptations; knowing this, that the trying of your faith works patience. But let patience have her perfect work, that you may be perfect and entire, lacking in nothing."*
This is a very important measure needed to face any kind of challenge. Whatever cannot be avoided must be endured; you are already in it and you will have to persist until you are out of it. Psalm 34:19-20 says *"Many are the afflictions of the righteous, but the Lord delivers him out of them all; He keeps his bones, not one of them is broken."*

Even our Lord Jesus Christ –the Author and Finisher of our faith– had to endure the hostility of sinners and the cross when He was here (Hebrews 12:2-4). The Bible was careful to present those facts about Jesus so that we will not become weary or faint in our minds when we face our own crosses.

If you know your afflictions are temporal, then endurance should become your watchword because weeping only lasts till the night; it never gets to the joyful morning.
Also, as good soldiers of Christ, you are expected to endure hardness (2 Timothy 2:3) while claiming what Jesus said in Luke 6:21 - *"...blessed are you that weep now, for you shall laugh"*. Please kindly endure, it will soon be over.

Look Beyond your Problem.
This measure was successfully applied by Joshua and Caleb in Numbers 13 and 14. The other men who went up with them to spy the land brought an evil report that they were like grasshoppers in the sight of the sons of Anak (the giants); but Joshua and Caleb said something else. They said *'let us go up at once and possess it; for we are well able to overcome it.'* Furthermore, they told the people: *"Fear not the people of the land, for they are bread for us; their defense is departed from them and the Lord is with us; fear them not."*

Did you see that? Two different reports concerning just one situation. Some saw peril, while the others who looked beyond the giants saw victory. It has been said that eyes that look are many but those that see are few. It was the evil report those men brought that led to their destruction in the wilderness while the positive minded ones went up, destroyed the giants and took over the land which flowed with milk and honey.

You need to see beyond your challenges if you are not going to be drowned by them. In Exodus 14: 1-14, when the children of Israel were thrown into confusion because of the Red Sea before them and the fast approaching Egyptian host, Moses looked beyond the problem and that decision created a way in the Red Sea for the first time.

They passed through; and at the end of the day, the Egyptian host they once saw, they saw no more.

You've got to develop a positive mentality about your situations. Never subscribe to pity or sympathy. You are more than what you are facing. None of the challenges you are faced with is superior to the grace of God upon your life. Keep your eyes on the things which are not seen (the eternal victory coming your way) and not on the pressures being generated by your present condition (2 Corinthians 4:18). This is what guarantees your coming forth as gold (Job 23:10).

Mind Your Speech.
Your confession in the time of your confusion is the conclusion of your condition. Matthew 12:37 says *"For by your words you shall be justified, and by your words you shall be condemned."*
This is where the devil cheats on many people. He would just suggest hopelessness; and if not discarded or renounced, it becomes part of your speech. As you confess it, it becomes registered, and it will definitely come to pass. Little wonder many people wallow in their predicaments without coming out; and some even die in them.

A very important story to illustrate this is that of the Israelites in the wilderness. They always murmured against God and Moses each time they faced seemingly difficult situations; but God would still show them mercy and give them whatever they needed. There were times when God wanted to deal with them, but upon hearing Moses' intercession for them, He would pardon them. This continued until a day came when their cup became full in Numbers 14:26-38. God said *"...say unto them, As truly as I live says the Lord, as you have spoken in my ears, so will I do to you, your carcasses shall fall in this wilderness and all that were numbered of you, according to your whole number from twenty years old and upward, who have murmured against me; doubtless, you shall not come into the land...except Caleb, the son of Jephunneh and Joshua, the son of Nun..."*

What a verdict!
You can read the entire Numbers 14 for a better understanding of this measure. They confessed destruction and they were utterly destroyed. Never say what you don't want to experience, because your words are creative.

If you say 'I'm finished', so be it. And if you say 'all is well', so be it. Learn not to take permanent decisions over temporal situations. Discipline your mouth to always say positive things no matter what you are passing through. Also, never murmur against your Creator – saying things like: **'Why Me?' 'What have I not done for You?' 'I pay my tithe, I go to church, I keep your sanctuary clean; what else do you want me to do?'**
Confessions like these will lengthen and compound your problems. Always remember that your confession (either positive or negative) is the conclusion of your condition; so watch your tongue.

Trust in God.
In any situation you find yourself in life, learn to exercise your faith by trusting solely in God. Proverbs 3:5-6 says *"Trust in the Lord with all your heart, and lean not on your own understanding. In all your ways, acknowledge Him, and He shall direct your paths."*
There is no person worthy of your trust, especially in times of trouble, other than God. Men are bound to disappoint, no matter how close they may appear to be; and that's why the Bible says woe unto the man who puts his trust in flesh – Jeremiah 17:5.

Habakkuk 2:4 says *"...but the just shall live by his faith."* And this manifested in the lives of the two blind men who trusted in Jesus' power to make them see as recorded in Matthew 9:27-30. Jesus touched their eyes and said to them *'according to your faith, be it unto you.'* And sure enough, they could see again.

Faith is **'not seeing, and yet believing.'** In fact, in this case **'believing is seeing'** as against the usual **'seeing is believing.'** It is faith that will keep you going even if the world is crashing on you, and it has never failed anyone before.

Hebrews 11:1-40 is a chapter to be carefully studied if the subject of faith is to be properly understood. Also, 1 John 5:4 which says *"For whoever is born of God overcomes the world; and this is the victory that overcomes the world, even our faith."*

I can therefore submit at this point that in exercising your faith when faced with any kind of challenge, your song should be like the one in Habakkuk 3:17-19 which says *"Although the fig tree shall not blossom, neither shall fruit be on the vines, the labor of the olive shall fail, and the field shall yield no food; the flock shall be cut off from the folds, and there shall be no herd in the stalls; yet I will rejoice in the Lord, I will joy in the God of my salvation. The Lord God is my strength, and He will make my feet like deer's feet; and He will make me walk upon my high places."*

Quickly Learn the Lessons.

A successful man is one who is able to build a strong house with the bricks others throw at him. There's always a lesson to learn from whatever happens to us; and until the lesson is learnt, the situation may persist.

If for instance, God allows some trials in your life so you can learn to look up to Him alone but you still go about seeking help from men, trusting their sweet promises; disappointments would be your constant experience. And until you grasp the lesson (trusting in God alone), you may keep on wallowing in various pools of disappointments. For example, David had to be afflicted in order to learn the statutes of God (Psalm 119:71).

When God is interested in you and you are paying little or no attention to Him, He may decide to use 'attention getters' like unanswered prayers, unemployment, disappointments, delay etc to pass His message across to you. And what's the message? Well, He might just be saying 'Turn to Me, I want to fellowship with you. I want to talk with you.' Or maybe He even wants to communicate an assignment He has for you.

I once heard of a woman who suffered a broken marriage for 16 years before God finally restored her home. And now, she is a marriage counselor. She is helping other marriages based on the lessons she has learnt. God doesn't waste any experience. He has a detailed curriculum for every individual He created.

So, each time you encounter a challenge, relax; don't be troubled. Try and find out the lessons you are expected to learn from it; grasp them as quick as possible and move on to the next level by applying the lessons accordingly. To say this in another way, whenever you fall, always make sure you pick up something from the ground.

Learn to Testify.

If God says He will with the temptations we face make a way of escape so that we can be able to bear it (1 Corinthians 10:13), it simply means He is faithful; and that should be made known.

Jesus Christ told His disciples that they would be His witnesses because they saw all the good things He did. But if the disciples had failed to tell us about those good things, we wouldn't know Jesus could save, heal, deliver, restore the broken-hearted, offer eternal life among many other benefits associated with His redemptive work on the cross. This shows the importance of sharing testimonies.

Testifying is all about telling others what God has done for you, even while you are still trusting Him to take care of the one you are currently facing. Look for something good to tell others about your God's faithfulness to you. If you are barren, testify about the gift of life; testify about the forgiveness of your sins and His promise to make you fruitful which you are very sure He would keep (Numbers 23:19).

Four things usually happen when you testify like this.

1. You become strengthened to trust God the more,
2. Your listeners (who may be facing something similar) are encouraged,
3. The devil becomes confused and frustrated by your uncommon attitude, and
4. The Almighty God moves into action to ensure you have more testimonies to share in order for Him to keep enjoying the glory. This He does by answering your prayers.

Build up your Spirit Man.

Though all problems and challenges of life have expiry dates, yet they don't occur once and for all; they usually occur in stages.

For instance, the challenge a man faces when he is 18 years old will not necessarily be the same he would face when he is 30 years old. As he keeps growing both physically and spiritually, he would encounter various challenges; and to keep experiencing victory in all of them, he would have to build up his spirit man – that is, an internal resistance and victory producing system. It would be very disgusting if he cried over his problems at 18 and he's still crying over them at 30. By now he's expected to be more experienced at handling life's challenges. And as he continues in life, this ability is expected to get better.

To prevent sin-induced problems for instance, you will have to store up God's Word in your heart (Psalm 119:11); abstain from all appearance of evil (1 Thessalonians 5:22); and you will have to ruthlessly deal with your flesh (1 Corinthians 9:27, Romans 13:14).

Let your spirit man grow by engaging in intensive Bible study, Biblical meditation, fasting and prayer among other relevant spiritual exercises. With a strong spirit, you will be able to withstand any challenge of life no matter how long it lasts. And at the end, you will come out excellently victorious. Proverbs 24:10 says *"If you faint in the day of adversity, your strength is small."*

So, start feeding on all the resources capable of building up your spirit – Christian tapes, CDs, Books, Bibles, Sermons etc. You can also visit our Facebook Page [**https://www.facebook.com/gloem.org**] and our Blog page [**https://gloem.org/my-blog**] for great resources capable of developing your spiritual stamina. These will help you become an overcomer regardless of what comes your way.

PRAYER POINTS

1. Father, thank You for opening my eyes to the truths contained in this book.
2. Father, please cause all my tormentors to hear a noise and leave me alone.
3. I cancel everything contrary to my glorification in Jesus' Name.
4. God of all possibilities, please cause my grass to become green again.
5. From today, my miracles shall no longer be delayed in Jesus' Name.
6. Father, beginning from now, let no man be able to trouble me and my family again in the Name of Jesus.
7. Father, I thank You for answering all my prayers. Glory be to Your Holy Name. Hallelujah!

BECOME A FINANCIAL PARTNER WITH JESUS

At *Global Emancipation Ministries - Calgary*, our mandate is *to liberate men through the knowledge of the Truth* and our mission statement is *creating channels through which men can encounter the Truth - [Isaiah 61:1-3; John 8:32, 36; I Thessalonians 5:24]*.

Our Ministerial Activities include Rural and Urban Evangelical Outreaches, Prison Evangelism, Hospital Ministrations, Mobilization for Missions Support, Teaching of the undiluted Word of God, Scripture-Based Seminars, Discipleship, Training of Field Missionaries and Empowerment of underprivileged ones among other Field Ministerial Tasks.

If you sense the Lord is calling you to reach out to the lost by engaging in any of these activities or by assisting those involved with your resources, please feel free to join us. Let us come together as we take the Gospel of our Lord Jesus Christ to the hurting and forgotten ones. [Mark 16:15-20].

Please join us in these kingdom projects by making your weekly, monthly, quarterly or annual donations to Global Emancipation Ministries – Calgary.

You can visit the "GIVE" section on our website, www.gloem.org, to learn about the ways to give.

For acknowledgement, please advise your donations to us by email: info@gloem.org or emancipation4souls@yahoo.com, and kindly include your details i.e. name, address, email and location. Alternatively, you can simply call +1 587 9735910 to do same.

You can also volunteer your gifts and talents in the service of the Lord through our ministerial platforms regardless of your location. To get information on how to go about this, please visit www.gloem.org and contact us via email: info@gloem.org or emancipation4souls@yahoo.com.

God bless you.

ABOUT THE AUTHOR

By the special grace of God, **Anthony O. Adefarakan** is the privileged President of **Global Emancipation Ministries - Calgary (GLOEM)** with headquarters in Canada, North America and **Emancipating Truth Ministry International (ETMI)** with headquarters in Nigeria, West Africa.

The Lord called him into the field ministry in February 2008 with the mandate to liberate men through the knowledge of the Truth, and by December 2012 he was ordained and commissioned as the Pioneer Pastor – in – Charge of The Redeemed Christian Church of God, Revelation Parish, Shalom Area under Delta Province III, Nigeria where he served until 1st February 2015 when he officially handed over to a new Pastor in order to focus on his field ministry to which the Lord had earlier called him and for which the authority of the church had already prayed and released him to undertake.

On 29th September 2013, he was awarded a Post Graduate Diploma in Tent – Making Mission from the Redeemed Christian School of Missions, Nigeria (RECSOM, Asaba Campus) where he also had the privilege to train Pastors and Missionaries as a lecturer in 2017.

Since the commissioning of his field ministry in 2015 he has had the opportunity to lead his ministry officers to field ministrations in different Prisons, Hospitals, Orphanages, Rural communities, Camp settlements, Markets, Local churches among other places with great successes on all occasions – such as salvation of sinners, healing of the sick, financial empowerment of mission churches, provision of relief materials to the poor, provision of medical services to the underprivileged, baptism in the Holy Ghost, deliverance from demonic oppression, release of inmates just to mention a few - all to the glory of God Who alone is the Doer.

He is the author of other best-selling titles such as **The Law of Kinds, Learning From the Ants, The Immutability of God's Counsel, Surely there is an End, Life Applicable lessons from the Book of Ruth, One thing is Needful Weekly Devotional Guide, Life Applicable Revelations from God's Word** (**Volumes 1 and 2**) among others.

He is blissfully married to Ifeoluwa A. Adefarakan and their marriage is fruitful to the glory of God.

Jesus is his Message, Freedom is the Outcome!
Isaiah 61:1-3

www.ingramcontent.com/pod-product-compliance
Lightning Source LLC
Chambersburg PA
CBHW041217070526
44583CB00001B/14